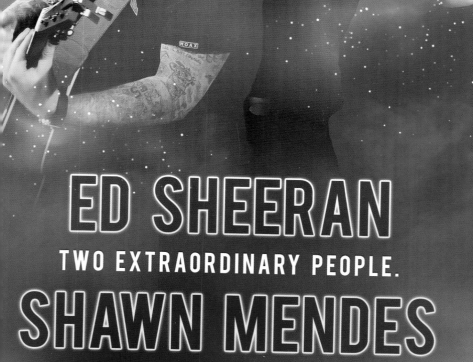

ED SHEERAN
TWO EXTRAORDINARY PEOPLE.
SHAWN MENDES

CONNECTED LIVES™

Ariana Grande | Camila Cabello

Ed Sheeran | Shawn Mendes

Halsey | Billie Eilish

John Legend | Michael Bublé

Kacey Musgraves | Maren Morris

Kane Brown | Sam Hunt

Kendrick Lamar | Travis Scott

Nicki Minaj | Cardi B

Photo credits: page 4: yakub88/Shutterstock.com; page 5: Andreas Rentz via Getty Images; page 7: JStone/ Shutterstock.com; page 8: Jason Merritt / iHeartMedia via Getty Images; page 9: Theo Wargo via Getty Images, Noam Galai via Getty Images; page 10: AlanWrigley via Alamy Stock Photo; page 11: Matt Winkelmeyer via Getty Images; page 12: Dan Kitwood via Getty Images; page 13: Ari Perilstein / Fabletics via Getty Images; page 16: Adam Berry via Getty Images; page 17: Kevork Djansezian via Getty Images; page 18: Phil Walter via Getty Images; page 19: Kevin Winter / iHeartMedia via Getty Images; page 20: Jamie McCarthy via Getty Images; page 21: Mike Coppola via Getty Images; page 22: Scott Gries via Getty Images; page 23: Willowtreehouse/Shutterstock.com; page 28: Ian Gavan via Getty Images; page 29: Kevin Winter via Getty Images; page 30: Stuart C. Wilson via Getty Images, Larry Busacca / Songwriters Hall Of Fame via Getty Images; page 31: Matt Winkelmeyer via Getty Images, Christopher Polk / Spotify via Getty Images; page 32: Noam Galai via Getty Images; page 34: Samir Hussein via Getty Images; page 36: Dave Thompson / WPA Pool via Getty Images; page 37: Andrew Parsons / WPA Pool via Getty Images; page 38: Dimitrios Kambouris / Verizon via Getty Images; page 40: Samir Hussein via Getty Images; page 41: Sonia Recchia via Getty Images; page 42: Kevork Djansezian via Getty Images; page 43: Kevin Winter / iHeartMedia via Getty Images; page 44: Gareth Cattermole via Getty Images; page 45: Kevin Winter via Getty Images; page 46: Michael Loccisano via Getty Images; page 47: Kevin Winter via Getty Images; page 48: John Phillips / Ed Sheeran via Getty Images; page 49: Andrew Toth via Getty Images; page 52: Ian Gavan via Getty Images; page 53: Brad Barket / Atlantic Records via Getty Images; page 54: Jason Davis / Americana Music via Getty Images; page 55: Kevin Winter / LiveNation via Getty Images; page 56: Gareth Cattermole via Getty Images; page 57: Rich Fury via Getty Images; page 58: Anna Webber / Atlantic Records via Getty Images; page 59: Tim Boyles / TAS via Getty Images, Kevin Winter / TAS via Getty Images; page 60: Gareth Cattermole via Getty Images; page 61: Dimitrios Kambouris via Getty Images, Michael Ochs Archives via Getty Images; page 62: Kevin Winter / Coachella via Getty Images, Ian Gavan via Getty Images; page 63: Kevin Winter / iHeartMedia via Getty Images; page 65: Gareth Cattermole via Getty Images, Kevin Winter / iHeartMedia via Getty Images; background: Chris Wong / EyeEm via Getty Images; Shawn Mendes head shot: JStone/ Shutterstock.com; Ed Sheeran head shot: DFree/Shutterstock.com

ISBN: 978-1-68021-789-6
eBook: 978-1-64598-075-9

Printed in Malaysia

24 23 22 21 20   1 2 3 4 5

TABLE OF CONTENTS

CHAPTER 1

EARLY LIFE

WHO IS ED SHEERAN?

Ed Sheeran is an English singer-songwriter. He performs with an acoustic guitar and no band. The singer was born in February 1991. Ed grew up in Framlingham, Suffolk. This is a small town in eastern England. Fewer than 4,000 people live there.

WHO IS SHAWN MENDES?

Shawn Mendes is a Canadian singer. Like Ed Sheeran, he writes his own songs. The singer was born in Toronto, Ontario, in August 1998. His parents raised him in Pickering, a suburb of Toronto. He told *Rolling Stone* that it is "the most comforting place in the world." Even after becoming a star, Shawn lived at home.

Ross Castle, Ireland

THE SHEERAN FAMILY

Ed's father, John Sheeran, is the son of Irish immigrants. The family visited Ireland often when the star was young. Irish culture, art, and music are important to the Sheerans. While Ed was growing up, his parents ran an art business.

THE MENDES FAMILY

Shawn's family has immigrant roots too. His father's grandparents came from Portugal. The Mendes family still visits Portugal to see relatives. In Toronto, Shawn's father sells restaurant supplies. Mrs. Mendes works as a real estate agent. She was born in England. "They are both entrepreneurs, which is awesome, and now I am one too," Shawn told the *Telegraph*.

Porto, Portugal

CANADIAN MUSICIANS

Many Canadian musicians make it big in the United States and around the world. Drake and Justin Bieber are both from Canada. So is R&B star The Weeknd. Canadian indie band Arcade Fire won a Grammy for Album of the Year in 2011. Megastar Celine Dion continues to entertain fans around the world.

Celine Dion

THE YOUNGER BROTHER

Ed has an older brother named Matthew. He is a composer. Matthew also plays violin and viola. Their grandmother's final wish was for the two boys to work together. In 2017, Matthew planned the music for one of Ed's songs. "It's quite a cool thing to work with your sibling," Ed said in an interview with Steve Wazz at Duke University.

sound wave tattoo

AN OLDER BROTHER

Shawn has a sibling too. His sister, Aaliyah, is five years younger. The two were very close growing up. Aaliyah recorded many of Shawn's early videos. The siblings have also recorded themselves singing together. "We have a really awesome connection," Shawn told KISS-FM radio. He even has a tattoo inspired by her. His sister and parents were recorded saying "I love you." This was turned into a drawing of a sound wave. Then Shawn got a tattoo of it.

Rishworth School

SCHOOL STRUGGLES

Ed grew up in a middle-class family. They sent him to a private school called Rishworth School. Teachers have described Ed as shy and quiet. His stutter and thick glasses made him a target of bullying. The singer talked about this in an interview with British rapper Dave and DJ Nihal. He said he "would cry every single day."

A FUN CHILDHOOD

Shawn's childhood was easier than Ed's. He had no problems at school and enjoyed playing sports. Hockey, soccer, and longboarding with friends were favorites. His family loved to have fun together too. "My dad takes Halloween serious," the singer told PopBuzz. "At our house we always dress up and create scenes. . . . It takes like three weeks. It was always a fun thing as a kid."

NO DIRECTION

Ed comes from an artistic and creative family. The star's father worked in the art world for 35 years. His mother makes jewelry. When Ed was growing up, the family did not have a TV. Paintings and sculptures filled their home. Ed and his brother were encouraged to draw, paint, or build with Legos. Becoming a musician was not yet in Ed's plans though.

THE ACTING BUG

As a child, Shawn did not want to be a musician either. He wanted to be an actor. His parents sent him to acting classes. Nerves got the best of him at a Disney Channel audition. The lines flew out of his head. "I walked in and . . . my hands were shaking," he told Beats 1 radio. Singing soon became his new goal.

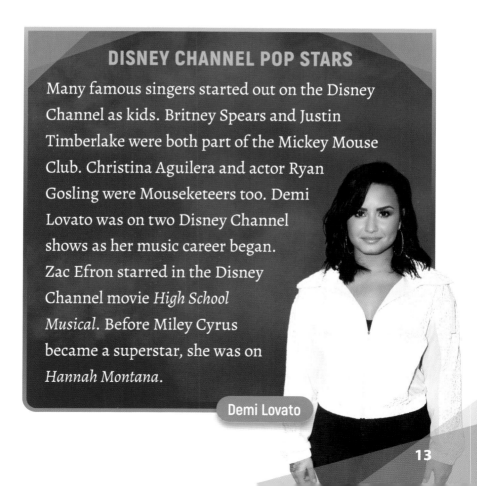

DISNEY CHANNEL POP STARS

Many famous singers started out on the Disney Channel as kids. Britney Spears and Justin Timberlake were both part of the Mickey Mouse Club. Christina Aguilera and actor Ryan Gosling were Mouseketeers too. Demi Lovato was on two Disney Channel shows as her music career began. Zac Efron starred in the Disney Channel movie *High School Musical*. Before Miley Cyrus became a superstar, she was on *Hannah Montana*.

Demi Lovato

A FAMILY INFLUENCE

From the age of four, Ed sang in a Catholic church choir. His mother sang there too. She is known for her voice. Ed's grandmother was also a singer. Benjamin Britten had her sing for him. He was a famous composer. When the boys were young, Ed's brother, Matthew, was a serious singer.

DISCOVERING HIS LOVE OF MUSIC

Unlike Ed's family, Shawn's did not have a musical background. They did not play instruments. Going to concerts was not a family activity. Still, Shawn's love of music started early. In fourth grade, he would watch YouTube videos for hours. Shawn would imitate cover songs posted by YouTubers. Doing this helped him learn how to sing.

ED SHEERAN

1. **Hebden Bridge, West Yorkshire:** Ed was born in this small town.

2. **Framlingham, Suffolk:** He spent his childhood here.

3. **London:** To make it in music, he moved here alone as a teenager.

SHAWN MENDES

4. **Pickering, Ontario:** Shawn spent his childhood here.

5. **Algarve region, Portugal:** His father's family is from this area.

6. **Toronto, Ontario:** This is where the first professional performance of his career took place.

CHAPTER 2

INTRO TO MUSIC

BREAKING AWAY

From a young age, Ed's brother was a promising violinist. In fact, the family moved to Framlingham partly for Matthew's music opportunities. Ed played the cello and piano when he was young. However, classical music was never his passion.

PUTTING HIMSELF OUT THERE

Shawn joined the glee club at his middle school. Glee club is like a school choir. He says that the club sparked his interest in singing. In eighth grade, his friends encouraged him to start performing online. Then, in 2012, Shawn posted his first video. It was a cover of Adele's "Hometown Glory." A childhood friend played piano while Shawn sang.

BUILDING CONFIDENCE

Ed began playing guitar in elementary school. At first, he taught himself. Then Ed took weekly lessons. Guitarist Keith Krykant was his teacher. As Ed's guitar skills grew, so did his confidence. Learning the Eminem song "Stan" helped him overcome his stutter. In high school, Ed started a band called Rusty. Classmates Fred and Rowley Clifford joined him. They played covers of rock songs.

WORKING AT IT

Shawn continued to post videos on YouTube. At first, he was not very skilled. "Watching back, it's super rough. I'm out of key. Everything's really bad," Shawn told *Billboard*. He was obsessed though. To improve, the singer listened to himself. Slowly but surely, he got better. Vocal lessons helped Shawn, just as guitar lessons helped Ed.

FINDING HIS DIRECTION

Ed was having fun with music, but he was not yet serious about it. His father told him he needed to find a direction and work hard. They began going to live shows together. Soon, Ed found his motivation. He wanted to be a professional musician.

LEARNING THE GUITAR

Around age 13, Shawn picked up an acoustic guitar. Similar to Ed, he discovered the instrument on his own. Someone had given it to his father. Shawn loved it and asked for a new one. His father said they could rent one first. If Shawn stuck with it, he could get a new one. The singer taught himself to play by watching YouTube videos. One of the first songs he learned was "The A Team" by Ed Sheeran.

GETTING INSPIRED

When Ed was in middle school, his dad took him to see Damien Rice. The singer-songwriter was performing at Whelan's, a famous pub in Dublin, Ireland. Rice was Ed's greatest inspiration. After the show, the two met. Rice was kind. He inspired the young musician to write his own songs. "I got home that night and wrote a whole bunch of songs and that is where the whole thing started," Ed told the *Telegraph*. Later, Ed got a tattoo of Rice's name on his arm.

DAMIEN RICE

Damien Rice is an alternative singer-songwriter from Ireland. Unlike Ed, Rice is shy of the spotlight. He is unconcerned with record sales and fame. The songwriter's 2002 album *O* was platinum four times over and was top ten in the United Kingdom. In 2006, his album *9* reached top five in the United Kingdom. Rice then took a break from music, going eight years before releasing his third album.

Damien Rice

PUSHING HIMSELF TO PERFORM

Shawn was posting many covers of songs on YouTube. However, he still hadn't performed offline. One of his first public performances was spur-of-the-moment. It was at a plaza in Portugal. "I was sweating," Shawn said to the *Guardian*. "I thought, Dude, if you want to be a singer, you've got to at least be able to stand on this statue and sing." The 13-year-old jumped up next to the statue. He sang a Bruno Mars song.

Lisbon, Portugal

EARLY RELEASES

Ed made his first album in 2004. *Spinning Man* was named after a picture his father owned. Not many copies of it exist. On January 1, 2005, Ed self-released his first EP, or short album. *The Orange Room* was its name. That was the color of his bedroom. When he made *The Orange Room*, Ed was 13. At this same age, Shawn began learning guitar. Ed's second full album was released the next year. Its title was *Ed Sheeran*. Fans found Ed on MySpace. That was where he shared his music.

TEENS & YOUTUBE

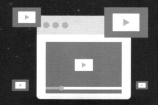

In 2018, YouTube was the **most popular website** among teenagers.

Almost half of teenagers told Pew Research they were online "almost constantly."

STILL IN THE HIGH SCHOOL WORLD

Ed's social life improved when he started playing music. However, Shawn's got worse. When Shawn was in ninth grade, he posted one of his early YouTube covers. The next day, he was walking down the hall. A group of older students teased him. "Sing for me!" they said. He later wrote on Instagram that it made him "feel like a joke." His core group of friends stood by him. They encouraged him to keep singing.

About **85 percent** of teens use YouTube.

The *New York Times* analyzed when people find their favorite music. The songs people discover in their **early teen years** are what they love most later on.

Many young YouTube musicians post original music. They receive **millions of views** from young fans. These artists never need to be "discovered" by the mainstream industry.

FULLY COMMITTED

Ed soon knew he only wanted to make music. Between 2007 and 2016, the singer says he never took a day off. He wrote music or performed every day. His parents helped him make professional albums and merchandise. They also took him to local gigs. "As a teenager my first dream was to make enough money from music to pay the rent and sell 100 CDs," he told *GQ UK*.

GOOFING AROUND

While Ed had ambitions, Shawn's music life was mostly for fun at first. In early 2013, Shawn joined the now-defunct social media site Vine. This site allowed users to upload six-second videos. These short clips played on a loop. Shawn's first videos on the platform were the kind of videos many teens post. A shot of his face in a dark room was his first Vine. "My #firstpost on Vine," the caption read.

PARALLEL LIVES

Bullied in school

Has an older brother

Family was musical

From England

Born in the 1990s

Middle-class upbringing

Sibling is also into music and performing

Got started by singing at school

Plays guitar

Played sports

School was pretty easy for him

Has a younger sister

From Canada

CHAPTER 3

RISE TO SUCCESS

MOVING TO LONDON

In April 2008, Ed took one step closer to fame. He persuaded Nizlopi to let him open for their show. They are a famous English folk duo. After his performance, he sold 20 of his own CDs. To him, that was a lot. It felt like a sign to keep focusing on music. Moving to London was the next step in Ed's career.

While living in London, Ed went to a music college. It was the Academy of Contemporary Music. During his first year, he was asked to open for the musician Just Jack. After that, Ed quit school for good. He performed in 312 shows in 2009, all while recording and releasing music.

Just Jack

OVERNIGHT SENSATION

Shawn did not need to move to London to find fame. He didn't even need to leave his house. YouTube, Instagram, Twitter, and Vine all saw frequent posts from him in 2013. That August, he covered Justin Bieber's "As Long as You Love Me" on Vine. He'd never posted music on the platform before. Aaliyah recorded the video. By the next morning, the cover had gone viral. Ten thousand users liked it overnight. It kept getting more popular. This was the beginning of the "six-second cover."

Justin Bieber

GRASSROOTS GROWTH

Ed continued working to be a professional musician. Fans found him at shows and online. He was also very popular on social media. "There's never been a point where it stalled," Ed told the *Mercury News*. "When I started off, I was getting love for what I was doing—just not a massive amount of it." In 2010, a rapper named Example saw a video Ed posted. Example took him on tour. With the addition of hip-hop fans, Ed's grassroots fan base grew even more.

Example

Lana Del Rey

CLIMBING THE VINE

Shawn realized almost no one else was using Vine for music. "You only have six seconds to impress somebody. And if you can . . . you've done a good job," he told the *New York Times*. The singer kept covering popular songs. He played hits from Taylor Swift, One Direction, and Lana Del Rey. It had been less than a year since he started playing guitar. Still, he gained millions of views and followers within months. People loved Shawn's look, sweetness, and voice.

HOLLYWOOD HUSTLE

Ed was still trying to get mainstream attention. In 2010, he flew to Los Angeles. The young singer only had one contact there, at a poetry open mic. His plan was to play open mic shows and sleep at friends' houses. Many labels rejected him. One night, he played at Jamie Foxx's club. Afterward, Foxx asked Ed to appear on his SiriusXM radio show. The star even let Ed live with him for six weeks. This was before Ed had a major record deal.

REAL FANS

Shawn wanted to move forward in his career too. Like Ed a few years earlier, he needed to take some risks. One day in October 2013, Shawn asked his fans a question on Twitter. "Hey, how many of you guys would come to a concert of mine if I did one in Toronto?" Many fans said they would. On October 26, he performed his first concert. Around 600 people attended. It was only a couple of months after his first popular Vine post.

MAGCON

Short for "Meet and greet convention," the first Magcon tour took place from 2013 to 2014. It featured a group of teenage social media stars, including Shawn. He left the tour in April 2014. Up to 2,000 fans paid to see the stars as they gave autographs and did shows. Founder Bart Bordelon called it "a boy-band phenomenon without the band." The group was revived for a worldwide tour in 2016 with some of the original stars. Other social media tours like YouTube's DigiTour followed.

FINALLY MAKING IT

In January 2011, Ed released another EP. It was his last without a record deal. This was his fifth EP and eighth release so far. Many British grime artists were featured on *No. 5 Collaborations Project*. Grime is a kind of hip-hop that started in England. The record reached number two on the British iTunes Chart. No label had promoted it. This gained wide attention. Ed's career took off. The rising star signed on with Atlantic Records soon after.

SCORING A CONTRACT

In 2014, manager Andrew Gertler was searching for a song on YouTube. It was "Say Something" by A Great Big World. Shawn's version was the first result to come up. Gertler loved it. He sent the link to someone at Island Records. They flew Shawn and his father to New York City. Executives listened to Shawn in the studio. "He was so naturally talented," Gertler told *Rolling Stone*.

New York City

BREAKTHROUGH

Atlantic Records put out Ed's breakthrough single in 2011. This was "The A Team." It sold 58,000 copies in a week. Ed received his first Grammy nomination for the song. He performed "The A Team" at Queen Elizabeth's 2012 Diamond Jubilee Concert. Once Ed had slept on the street outside Buckingham Palace after playing a show. Now he was there performing for royalty.

Queen Elizabeth's 2012 Diamond Jubilee

STILL IN SCHOOL

Shawn had been named a "Face of the Future" by his high school in 2013. The prediction was proven right. After his junior year of high school, Shawn left to go on tour. He opened for singer Austin Mahone. Pine Ridge Secondary allowed him to finish the rest of his classes online. In June 2016, he graduated with his class.

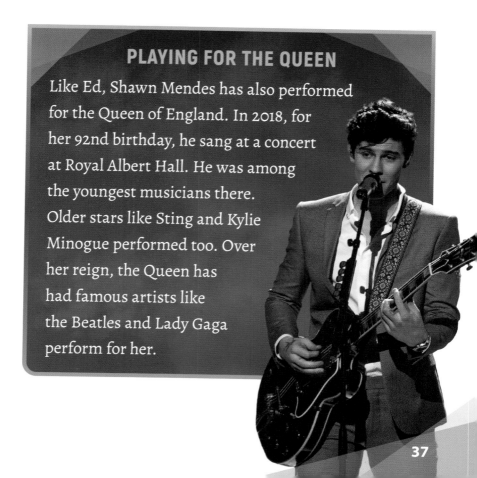

PLAYING FOR THE QUEEN

Like Ed, Shawn Mendes has also performed for the Queen of England. In 2018, for her 92nd birthday, he sang at a concert at Royal Albert Hall. He was among the youngest musicians there. Older stars like Sting and Kylie Minogue performed too. Over her reign, the Queen has had famous artists like the Beatles and Lady Gaga perform for her.

EARLY RECEPTION

Ed had major talent. But he was known for being a regular, down-to-earth guy. This image showed up in his song lyrics too. His songs were always very personal. Fans could relate to them. Fellow singers praised Ed's work ethic and collaborative spirit. They also admired his skill on guitar.

JUST FOR KIDS?

Early on, Shawn's fan base was mainly teenage girls. Adult music reviewers were more critical. Still, they enjoyed his early work. *Pitchfork* said he was like "the cutest counselor at your summer camp." Everyone agreed that Shawn was polite and grounded. Soon, he would be praised for his songwriting skills.

CAREER MILESTONES

1991
Ed is born in Halifax, England.

1998
Shawn is born in Ontario, Canada.

2004
Spinning Man is recorded. This is the first of several self-released albums by Ed.

2008
Ed moves to London and starts performing.

2011
Ed's first studio album, + (Plus), is released. It reaches number one in the United Kingdom and number five in the U.S.

2013
Shawn starts posting on Vine.

2014
His first self-titled EP is released.

2015
Shawn's first album, *Handwritten,* is released. He is the youngest artist to debut at number one on Billboard since Justin Bieber.

2017
÷ (Divide) is released. It reaches number one in both countries. Ed begins a two-year world tour.

2018
"In My Blood" tops the Billboard Adult Pop Songs chart. Shawn becomes the first and only artist to have four number-one singles in the chart before he turns 20 years old.

2019
Ed releases *No. 6 Collaborations Project,* which reaches number one in the United Kingdom.

2019
The single "If I Can't Have You" debuts at number two in the U.S. Billboard Hot 100, becoming his highest-charting single on the list.

CHAPTER 4

STARDOM

FIRST ALBUM

Ed released his debut studio album, + (Plus), in September 2011. It was a major success. The album sold more than a million copies in six months. This was just in England. Three of the singles from + were top five on Britain's singles chart. Reaching number five in the U.S., the album stayed in the charts for years.

FIRST SINGLE

In fall 2014, Shawn's debut single, "Life of the Party," hit number 24 on the Billboard Hot 100. At 15, Shawn was the youngest artist ever to have a song debut in the top 25. "Life of the Party" sold more than 150,000 copies in its first week. His existing online fan base was the reason. The song did not have the lasting success of Ed's first album. Radio stations ignored the single. However, it still managed to go platinum.

FIRST GRAMMY WIN

Ed's next album, × (Multiply), appeared in June 2014. It debuted at number one in both the U.S. and England. The single "Sing" was Ed's first number-one hit in England. There were three other top ten singles on ×. These included "Don't," "Photograph," and "Thinking Out Loud." Spotify named Ed the most-streamed artist in the world for 2014. In 2015, "Thinking Out Loud" won Grammys for Song of the Year and Best Pop Solo Performance.

SINGING FALSETTO

Both musicians use falsetto, which is a high tone of voice. It is similar to something called head voice, but breathier. In both, sound vibrates in the head instead of the chest or diaphragm. If you talk like Mickey Mouse, this is using your head voice. If you yodel, you are switching between head and chest voice.

A RAPID RISE

Shawn released his first EP with Island Records in 2014. The *Shawn Mendes EP* was even bigger than "Life of the Party" had been. It reached the number-one spot on iTunes in 37 minutes. The album also went straight to number five in the U.S. In 2014, Shawn's rapid rise landed him on *Time* magazine's Most Influential Teens list. He made that list three more times in the following years.

STAYING ON TOP

In 2016, Ed took a break from performing. He worked on his third studio album, ÷ (Divide). In January 2017, he released two singles from the album. These were "Shape of You" and "Castle on the Hill." They both debuted in the top ten. Ed is the first artist in U.S. history to have this happen.

FIRST TOUR AND ALBUM

Shawn began touring soon after signing with his record label. After his tour with Austin Mahone, he began a year-long tour for his EP. That was in fall 2014. *Handwritten* was released in April 2015. This first full-length album was made in just five months. Just like Ed did with ÷, Shawn broke a record. *Handwritten* debuted at number one on the Billboard 200. Shawn was the youngest artist to accomplish this since Justin Bieber.

Austin Mahone

BREAKING RECORDS

With ÷, Ed became a true superstar. The album was released in March 2017. It broke a Spotify record for first-day album streams. Worldwide, ÷ was named the top-selling album of 2017. The single "Shape of You" was in the top ten for 33 straight weeks. This was the longest-ever run in history. "Shape of You" is the most-streamed song ever on Spotify. Viewers have watched the video for the song more than 4 billion times on YouTube.

2017 MTV Music Awards

People's Choice Awards 2016

STEPPING INTO STARDOM

Shawn found his own stardom with his second album, *Illuminate*. He also found his voice. The September 2016 album listed him as a songwriter on every song. "This time, I knew I would be standing next to the producer the whole time and making sure it was exactly what I wanted," Shawn told AXS. "We captured this new, inner voice that I had no idea I even had." The album topped the charts. Tickets for the *Illuminate* tour sold out in minutes.

SUPERSTAR

Ed has become one of the best-selling musicians in the world. He has won four Grammys. One of his shows at Madison Square Garden sold out in three minutes. London's 80,000-seat Wembley Stadium was sold out three nights in a row. The star has not used Twitter since 2017. Still, more than 19 million people follow him there. Nearly 32 million people follow him on Instagram. His personal life is also thriving. Ed announced in 2019 that he'd married Cherry Seaborn. The couple met in high school.

Wembley Stadium

STAYING POWER

Shawn released his third album in 2018. It was called *Shawn Mendes*. The next year, his single "If I Can't Have You" became a huge success. That year, he went on yet another world tour. Touring is something Shawn is used to now. The singer sleeps better on his tour bus than in hotels. On Twitter, more than 23 million fans follow him. More than 50 million follow him on Instagram. The star has been nominated for two Grammys. He has also won Teen Choice Awards and MTV Europe Music Awards.

STREAMING STARS

As of July 2019, the two artists topped the list of Spotify artists with the most monthly listeners. Ed Sheeran was number one, with 69.65 million listeners per month. Shawn Mendes was number two, with 56.48 million.

GIVING BACK

Ed says all he wants is enough money to be comfortable. In 2014, he donated many of his clothes to thrift stores. Much of his money goes to children's hospitals. Family and friends also receive generous gifts. The star raises money playing shows and recording music. Ed was part of Band Aid 30 in 2014. It raised money for the Ebola crisis in western Africa.

EQUIVALENT ALBUM SALES
(AS OF LATE 2018)

Fans buy physical copies and digital copies of an album. They also stream the album and its songs. Digital purchases are another way fans can listen to albums. Equivalent Album Sales add up all of these ways of accessing music.

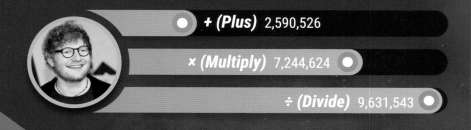

+ (Plus) 2,590,526

× (Multiply) 7,244,624

÷ (Divide) 9,631,543

A FORCE FOR GOOD

Shawn helps people too. One way is through social media. He raised funds for the Red Cross after the 2017 Mexico City earthquake. Together with his label, the singer donated $100,000 to the cause. Through a campaign with DoSomething.org, Shawn aimed to raise kids' self-esteem. In 2015, he sold exclusive items to raise money to build a new school in Ghana. His #BuildASchoolWithShawn campaign reached its goal in only a week.

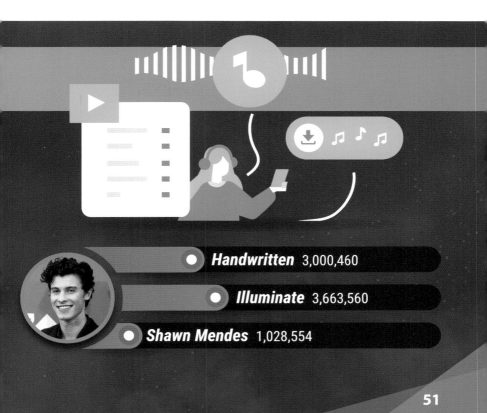

Handwritten 3,000,460

Illuminate 3,663,560

Shawn Mendes 1,028,554

CHAPTER 5

INFLUENCES AND COLLABORATIONS

A VARIED BUNCH

Many singer-songwriters and classic groups have influenced Ed. Joni Mitchell, Bob Dylan, and the Beatles are some of them. At age 11, Ed saw Eric Clapton play his song "Layla" on television. Soon after, he bought a guitar at a pawnshop. He told *People* that Clapton was "the reason I started playing guitar." Ed became obsessed with the instrument. Another influence was Nizlopi. The folk duo helped Ed learn how to perform live. They taught him to sing louder.

Eric Clapton

POP STARS

Shawn's family listened to reggae and country music when he was young. He doesn't quite remember the first album he bought. It may have been a Shania Twain or *Hannah Montana* album. The singer often names Justin Timberlake and Bruno Mars as strong influences on his music. Some people compare him to Justin Bieber. Both are Canadian and were discovered online. But their styles are very different.

Bruno Mars

VAN THE MAN

Van Morrison and the Chieftains' *Irish Heartbeat* was a very important early album for Ed. He loved traditional Irish music. Ed liked Van Morrison's blues style too. Later in his life, Ed would perform hits from *Irish Heartbeat* at concerts. They included "Carrickfergus" and "Raglan Road." The lyrics to "Shape of You" even mention Van the Man.

Van Morrison

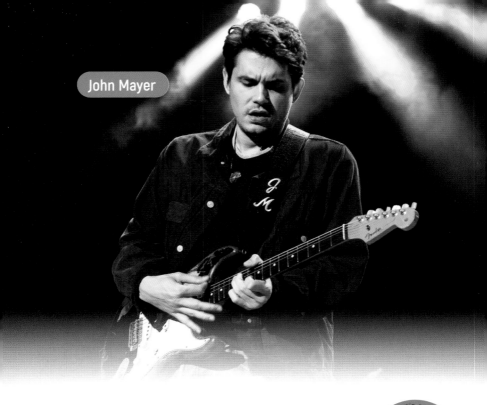

John Mayer

JOHN MAYER

Shawn admires a bluesy singer too. He likes John Mayer's songwriting and his blues style. *Illuminate* was influenced by Mayer's *Continuum*. The two are now friends. Shawn told *People* that "the most incredible thing I learned from [Mayer] is that no matter how much experience you have, you never are done learning." In 2017, Shawn performed with Mayer. The next year, Mayer came onstage to perform with Shawn.

Stormzy

HIP-HOP

Ed has long been popular with grime and rap stars.
Early on, Jamal Edwards invited Ed to perform on his
YouTube channel. Edwards is a popular grime musician.
Grime star Stormzy has also complimented Ed's rap
abilities. The singer-songwriter has worked with grime
rappers Wiley, Devlin, Sway, and Wretch 32. Ed has
also worked with American rappers. In 2019, Ed's idol
Eminem recorded a song with him.

ED SHEERAN

Just like Ed, Shawn has his own idols. One of them is Ed Sheeran. "I probably watched [a video of 'Gimme Love'] on replay for four hours until my mom was like, 'You have to turn that off; I can't hear it anymore,'" Shawn told Beats 1. In 2014, Ed saw some videos of Shawn. The older singer liked what he heard. He flew Shawn out to Los Angeles for dinner. Shawn told *Billboard* that at the meeting, "I forgot he's my idol. I felt like I was in the room with one of my buddies."

OVERCOMING OBSTACLES

Both artists had to deal with anxiety even after they were famous. Shawn first opened up about his anxiety in the hit song "In My Blood." It helps him to remember that everyone deals with some level of anxiety. A few therapy sessions helped too. Ed said social anxiety is a longtime obstacle. The star struggles to trust people. Focusing on his best friends helps him get through difficult situations.

MAKE IT SWIFT

Once he hit it big, Ed began cowriting songs with bigger artists. Some were One Direction and Taylor Swift. He has worked with Swift many times. Together, they wrote Swift's song "Everything Has Changed." It came out in 2012. Later, Ed opened for Swift on her 2013 RED arena tour. In 2017, the two made Swift's song "End Game." They are close friends.

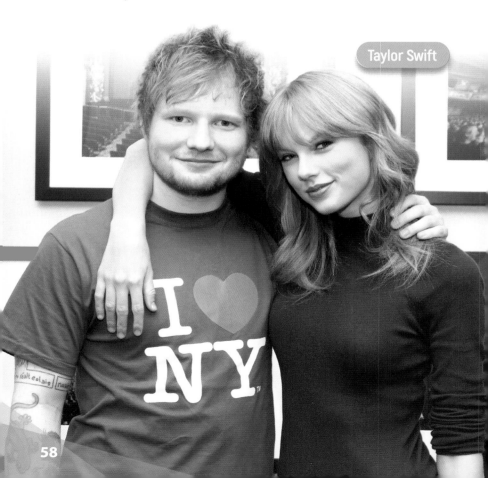

Taylor Swift

Taylor Swift

FRIEND IN COMMON

Shawn toured with Taylor Swift too. He joined her
on the 1989 World Tour. A lifelong fan, he became
friends with the megastar. She brought Shawn out on
a California stage in 2018. They sang a duet of his song
"There's Nothing Holding Me Back." In 2019, Shawn
wrote about his friend in *Time* magazine. The singer
pointed out Swift's "electrifying connection" to her fans.
He admires her talent for making young people "feel
they can do anything."

BRANCHING OUT

Ed acted in *Game of Thrones*. He played a Lannister soldier who sang a song while Arya stopped for a meal with his group. In the movie *Yesterday,* Ed played himself. The singer started his own label too. It is called Gingerbread Man Records. The label is part of Atlantic Records.

Ed with Lily James and Himesh Patel

SECRETS TO THEIR SUCCESS

Shawn is seen as a poster child for how to become a superstar in the social media era. He is relatable to fans and built a grassroots fan base online and through live shows. Ed didn't wait to be discovered. He only signed a record deal after he had a hit. Each artist is committed to their fans and driven to improve both musically and in business.

Elvis Presley

SEEKING NEW ROLES

Shawn started to act once he hit it big. The CW's *The 100* added him in a small role. This was after Shawn tweeted that he loved the show and would like to be on it. In 2019, Shawn said that he was looking through scripts and hoping to act in movies soon. Playing Elvis Presley is one cherished goal. The singer has also modeled for Calvin Klein Jeans.

STILL MAKING THE ROUNDS

Ed continues to work with many different artists. "I Don't Care" with Justin Bieber came out in May 2019. The song broke the single-day streaming record for Spotify. It was the first single from Ed's *No.6 Collaborations Project*. Another single from this album is "Beautiful People," with Khalid. Shawn collaborated with Khalid too. They wrote and recorded 2018's "Youth."

Khalid

CAMILA CABELLO

Shawn's most lasting musical partner is Camila Cabello. On a re-release of Shawn's *Handwritten*, the two sang "I Know What You Did Last Summer." It made the top 20 in the U.S. and Canada. They also cowrote and performed the hit song "Señorita." This was in June 2019. The song set a single-day record for a male-female duet on Spotify.

Camila Cabello

COLLABORATIONS

Ed brought **Shawn** to Los Angeles before his first album, in 2014.

Shawn covered **Ed's** songs online early on.

Ed joined **Shawn** onstage in 2017 to sing Shawn's "Mercy" together.

The **two singers** cowrote **Shawn's** song "Fallin' All in You."

Shawn has said: **"[Ed's]** whole style is not fake at all. . . . That's how I want to be."

CONNECTED LIVES

Like many modern pop stars, Ed and Shawn continue to grow in popularity by sharing their talents with other artists. Pop music today has more features and collaborations than ever before. This is partly due to the collaborative spirit of hip-hop, one of Ed's favorite genres. Perhaps in the future, Ed and Shawn will share space on the charts with a duet of their own.

TAKE A LOOK INSIDE

HALSEY

TWO EXTRAORDINARY PEOPLE.

BILLIE EILISH

CHAPTER 1

EARLY LIFE

WHO IS HALSEY?

Halsey is a singer and songwriter. Her given name is Ashley Nicolette Frangipane. She was born on September 29, 1994, in Clark, New Jersey. The star still visits her home state. New Jersey is "like a little sister or a little brother that's annoying . . . but I love you still," the singer told Business Insider.

WHO IS BILLIE EILISH?

Singer and songwriter Billie Eilish was born on December 18, 2001. Her parents named her Billie Eilish Pirate Baird O'Connell. The singer was named after her grandfather Bill. "Pirate was going to be my middle name," she told the BBC in 2017. "But then my uncle had a problem with it because pirates are bad. Then Baird is my mother's name." Billie was born in Los Angeles, California.

COLLABORATIONS AND POLITICS

In April 2019, Halsey was featured in "Boy with Luv." The song is by Korean boy band BTS. Their single had 74.6 million views on YouTube in one day. That is the most views ever in a single day.

Halsey has also been outspoken on politics and social issues. On Earth Day in April 2019, she and 29 others were featured on a Lil' Dicky single about climate change. The single was called "Earth." Billie speaks out on politics too. In 2018 she worked with the mayor of Los Angeles to get young people to vote.

ART AND MUSIC

Visual artists have long collaborated with and influenced musicians. Takashi Murakami has worked with other musicians, such as Pharrell, on music videos. Artist Jeff Koons designed Lady Gaga's *ArtPop* cover. Drake's "Hotline Bling" video was said to be influenced by artist James Turrell. Kanye West worked with performance artist Vanessa Beecroft on the creative production of his Yeezus Tour.

ALBUM STREAMS AS OF 2019

Badlands
Spotify 1,545,678,000
YouTube 989,300,000

hopeless fountain kingdom
Spotify 1,267,349,000
YouTube 826,700,000

When We All Fall Asleep, Where Do We Go?
Spotify 2,142,842,000
YouTube 1,372,100,000

BECOMING A DESIGNER

Spotify set up an "enhanced album experience" for Billie in 2019. Outside was a statue of Billie. World-famous Japanese artist Takashi Murakami designed it. Inside, there were 14 rooms. Each room was for a song on the album. Workers wore white jumpsuits. The jumpsuits were from Billie's fashion line. Called Blöhsh, the line's logo is a small green stick figure. Billie began by sketching outfits herself. She still helps design a lot of the clothing. It is inspired by the singer's streetwear style.

SWAGGER

Halsey has said that Kanye West, Brand New, and Bright Eyes are inspirations. She admires film directors like Quentin Tarantino and Larry Clark as well. The singer is influenced by the swagger and confidence of male musicians. "All the musicians I loved growing up were men," she said. Some of her favorites were Leonard Cohen, Mick Jagger, and Matty Healy from The 1975.

DISCOVERING HIP-HOP

Billie admires hip-hop. She loves that it is like poetry, with rhymes and references woven in. Similar to Halsey, many of her biggest influences are men. Childish Gambino's 2013 album *Because the Internet* was her introduction to rap, at age 11. Rapper Tyler, the Creator "changed the way she thinks" about music and fashion. Tyler, the Creator admires her too. He has said he would love to work with Billie.

TOP BILLBOARD HOT 100 SINGLES

● HALSEY

#1	Closer featuring The Chainsmokers	9/2016
#5	Bad at Love	1/2018
#9	Eastside featuring Benny Blanco, Khalid	1/2019
#1	Without Me	1/2019
#8	Boy with Luv featuring BTS	4/2019

● BILLIE EILISH

#14	Bury a Friend	2/2019
#31	Wish You Were Gay	4/2019
#29	When the Party's Over	4/2019
#35	Xanny	4/2019
#1	Bad Guy	8/2019

FOR MORE TITLES AND INFORMATION ⟶

CONNECTED LIVES™

ARIANA GRANDE
TWO EXTRAORDINARY PEOPLE.
CAMILA CABELLO

9781680217957

ED SHEERAN
TWO EXTRAORDINARY PEOPLE.
SHAWN MENDES

9781680217896

HALSEY
TWO EXTRAORDINARY PEOPLE.
BILLIE EILISH

9781680217919

JOHN LEGEND
TWO EXTRAORDINARY PEOPLE.
MICHAEL BUBLÉ

9781680217926

KACEY MUSGRAVES
TWO EXTRAORDINARY PEOPLE.
MAREN MORRIS

9781680217964

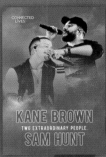

KANE BROWN
TWO EXTRAORDINARY PEOPLE.
SAM HUNT

9781680217902

KENDRICK LAMAR
TWO EXTRAORDINARY PEOPLE.
TRAVIS SCOTT

9781680217933

NICKI MINAJ
TWO EXTRAORDINARY PEOPLE.
CARDI B

9781680217940

MORE TITLES COMING SOON
SDLBACK.COM/CONNECTED-LIVES